Adventures of the Polar Bear Brothers

Happy House

About Wise & Wide

- A systematic 6-level English reading program based on Lexile® measures
- Diverse and interesting topics chosen from the elementary curriculums of Korea and English speaking western countries
- Well-written books in various forms including fiction stories, descriptive texts, and classics retold
- The informative but original fiction stories grab your interest, leading to the easy and clear understanding of the educational content.
- Improve thinking skills with solid after-reading activities at all levels of the series.

Wise & Wide is a 6-level English reading program that consists of 60 books and each level is systematically divided by Lexile® measures. The Lexile® Framework for Reading is the most popular reading measuring system in American formal education curriculums and many English programs. Over 20 out of 50 states in the U.S. mark Lexile® measures directly on students' final report cards and over 300 well-known publishers adopt and use Lexile® measures.

Experience many kinds of readings written by professional writers from the U.S. and England. They used interesting topics that were carefully chosen after analyzing elementary curriculums from around the world including Korea, the U.S., England, and Australia among many others. Comprehensive after-reading activities including graphic organizers, speaking tasks, and After-reading Tests are ready for you.

Levels in the series and their corresponding Lexile® measures

Level	Lexile® measures	U.S. Grade
Level 1	Below 200L	Pre K - K
Level 2	190L - 400L	Lower Grade 1
Level 3	350L - 530L	Upper Grade 1
Level 4	420L - 650L	Grade 2
Level 5	520L - 940L	Grade 3 - 4
Level 6	830L - 1070L	Grade 5 - 6

* Smart Readers: Wise & Wide level 1 is applicable to the preschool level in the U.S.
* The source of the relationship between Lexile® measures and U.S. school grades: CCSS(Common Core State Standards) FOR ENGLISH LANGUAGE ARTS, APPENDIX A (2012, which is used by 45 states in the U.S.)

Topic List

	Level 1	Level 2	Level 3	Level 4	Level 5	Level 6
Book 1	Science>Biology: The hibernation of animals Story	Science>Biology: Living and nonliving things Story	Science>Biology> Animals & the Environment: Sea otters Story	Environment> Living with nature: The diver & the persimmon tree Story	Science>Biology> Animal: Amazing animals of the Amazon Story	Science>Biology: Germs, transmitted diseases Story
Book 2	Literature> World classics: Aesop's fables Story	Literature> Traditional fairy tale: Old tales about stones Story	Social Studies> Economy: To run a business to make and save money Story	Science>Biology> Plants: Photosynthesis Story	Science>Earth science: Earth's layers, earthquakes, volcanoes, and earth's atmosphere Report	Mathematics> Sequence: The golden ratio & the Fibonacci sequence Story
Book 3	Science>Physics: How shadows are formed Story	Literature> World classics: Peter Pan Story	Science>Scientific technology: Nanobots Story	Literature>Myths: World's creation stories Story	Literature> Legend: The story of King Arthur Story	Literature>Myths: Constellation myths Story
Book 4	Literature> Traditional literature: The Talmud Story	Science>Biology> Animal: Polar bears Story	Science>Biology> Animal: Mountain gorillas Story	Social Studies> Cultural anthropology: Amazing ancient cultures of the world Story	Science> Earth science: Clouds and weather Story	Literature> Human & animals: The friendship between a girl and a horse Story
Book 5	Social Studies> Ethics: Rules in daily life Story	Science>Biology: The five senses Report	Social Studies> Cultural anthropology: Astonishing festivals Report	Art>Music: Stories from two operas Story	Social Studies> World culture & history: The Renaissance Story	Sports> Board sports: Surfing & snowboarding Story
Book 6	Social Studies> World geography & travel: Tourist attractions around the world Story	Science>Biology> Animal: Dinosaurs Story	Science> Astronomy: The solar system Story	Social Studies> People: Three great people who overcame hardships Story	Science>Scientific technology: The wonderful world of robots Report	Art>Music: Composers of the Romantic Era Report
Book 7	Science> Space science: The life of astronauts Report	Social Studies> Cultural anthropology: Mythological monsters from around the world Report	Mathematics> Elementary mathematics: Numbers, measurement, shapes and data Report	Science & Social Studies> Technology & culture: Inventions from around the world Report	Art>Works of art: Famous paintings Report	Social Studies> Human & animals: Animals in action for human Report
Book 8	Social Studies> Cultural anthropology: Various living cultures of the world Story	Art>Music: Instruments in the orchestra Story	Social Studies> Life safety: Learning and using outdoor survival skills Story	Social Studies> History: The California Gold Rush Report	Social Studies & Science> Psychology: Psychology in everyday life Story	Literature> World classics: The Merchant of Venice Story
Book 9	Social Studies> Jobs: Interviews about jobs Report	Science>Scientific technology: Developments in technology in different times Story	Social Studies> Politics>Election: Running for 3rd grade class president Story	Literature> World classics: Stories of Sherlock Holmes Story	Literature> World classics: Adrift in the Pacific Story	Social Studies> History & People: Great world leaders in history Report
Book 10	Literature>Traditional fairy tale: Eastern and Western folk tales on the same theme Story	Sports>Winter sports: Various aspects of some Winter Olympic sports Report	Literature> World classics: Short stories by O. Henry Story	Sports> Ball games: Various aspects of popular ball games Report	Social Studies> History: Famous events that changed world history Report	Art & Social Studies> Art: Stories about the creation, distribution, and preservation of paintings Report

How to Use This Book

•Before Reading

You can easily find the topic and what kind of story you are about to read.

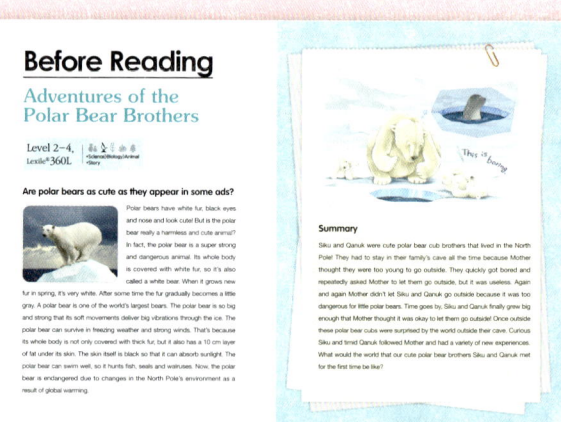

•The text

All the stories were written by professional writers from the U.S. and England, so you will read authentic and appropriate English sentences and expressions in every book in the series.

•Pop Quiz

Check out right away if you understand what you have just read by solving a pop quiz that checks your comprehension.

•Key Words

The key words and expressions on each page are listed for you to easily study them.

•Aha! Tips

Download free Korean explanations at *www.ihappyhouse.co.kr* for all of the sentences marked with "Aha!". These explain cultural, scientific, and economic knowledge or they deal with aspects of English such as grammatical structures or idiomatic expressions. There are lots of "Aha! Tips" to help you understand the text.

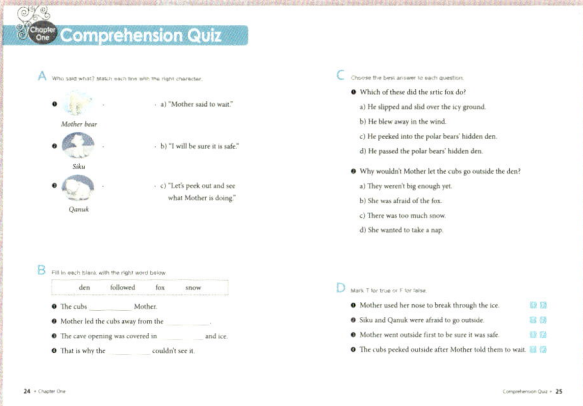

•Comprehension Quiz

After reading one chapter, solve various questions to find out if you fully understand the content.

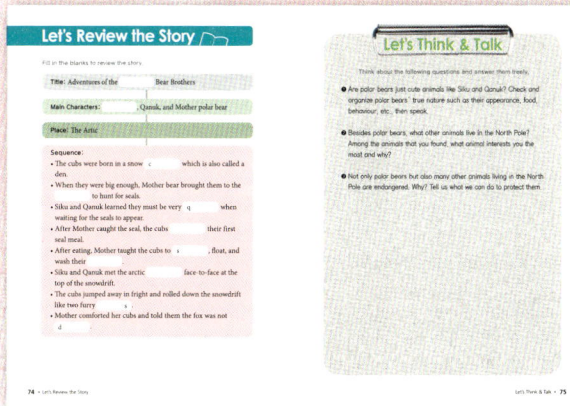

•Let's Review the Story /
•Let's Think & Talk

Fill in the blanks in the organizer to summarize the whole story. Express your own thinking and feelings about the story by answering the questions. You can build up logic and reasoning skills for your essay examinations in the future.

Appendix

Audio CD

In the CD audio book form, the texts are read vividly by American professional voice actors.

After-reading Test

Solve an additionally provided After-reading Test for each book.

The Korean translation, Answer Keys, a Word Quiz, a Word List, and Aha! Tips for each book

You can download them for free at *www.ihappyhouse.co.kr*

Before Reading

Adventures of the Polar Bear Brothers

Level 2–4,
Lexile® 360L

•Science〉Biology〉Animal
•Story

Are polar bears as cute as they appear in some ads?

Polar bears have white fur, black eyes and nose and look cute! But is the polar bear really a harmless and cute animal? In fact, the polar bear is a super strong and dangerous animal. Its whole body is covered with white fur, so it's also called a white bear. When it grows new fur in spring, it's very white. After some time the fur gradually becomes a little gray. A polar bear is one of the world's largest bears. The polar bear is so big and strong that its soft movements deliver big vibrations through the ice. The polar bear can survive in freezing weather and strong winds. That's because its whole body is not only covered with thick fur, but it also has a 10 cm layer of fat under its skin. The skin itself is black so that it can absorb sunlight. The polar bear can swim well, so it hunts fish, seals and walruses. Now, the polar bear is endangered due to changes in the North Pole's environment as a result of global warming.

Summary

Siku and Qanuk were cute polar bear cub brothers that lived in the North Pole! They had to stay in their family's cave all the time because Mother thought they were too young to go outside. They quickly got bored and repeatedly asked Mother to let them go outside, but it was useless. Again and again Mother didn't let Siku and Qanuk go outside because it was too dangerous for little polar bears. Time goes by, Siku and Qanuk finally grew big enough that Mother thought it was okay to let them go outside! Once outside these polar bear cubs were surprised by the world outside their cave. Curious Siku and timid Qanuk followed Mother and had a variety of new experiences. What would the world that our cute polar bear brothers Siku and Qanuk met for the first time be like?

Contents

Adventures of the Polar Bear Brothers

Adventures of the Polar Bear Brothers

Big Enough

The arctic wind blew cold.

Bits of ice and snow swirled in the air.

An arctic fox trotted over the icy ground.

The wind ruffled his white fur.

He passed a snow cave, but didn't see it.

It was hidden in a snowdrift.

Deep in the cave, two polar bear cubs lived with their mother.

▲ arctic fox

Outside the wind blew and it was cold.

Inside the hidden den, the cub brothers, Siku and Qanuk, stayed cozy.

KEY WORDS

- enough
- arctic
- **blow** (blow-blew-blown)
- bit
- swirl
- arctic fox
- trot
- icy
- ruffle
- fur

- pass
- cave
- **hide** (hide-hid-hidden)
- snowdrift
- deep
- cub
- **outside** (↔ inside)
- den
- stay
- cozy

Before Siku and Qanuk were born, Mother built the den. She chose a snowdrift on a slope. Her sharp claws dug into the ice.

She used her strong paws to move the snow.

Mother dug until she built a cave inside the snowdrift.

The thick walls of snow and ice kept the wind and cold out.

KEY WORDS

- be born
- build (build-built-built)
- choose (choose-chose-chosen)
- slope
- sharp
- claw
- dig (dig-dug-dug)
- paw
- until
- thick
- keep out (keep-kept-kept)
- rest
- alone
- mating
- prepare for
- raise
- care for

Then Mother rested alone in the den until Siku and Qanuk were born.

Polar bear parents do not stay together after mating.

The mother bear prepares for her cubs alone.

She raises them alone, too!

Siku and Qanuk's mother was happy to care for her cubs.

Siku and Qanuk were tiny at birth.

They weighed half a kilogram each.

That is only about the weight of one shoe!

But safe in the den, they grew.

Their fur grew thicker. Aha!

Their snouts grew longer.

Their paws grew bigger.

Their teeth and claws became sharper.

KEY WORDS

- tiny
- at birth
- weigh
- half
- kilogram (1kg= 1000g)
- each
- weight
- safe

- grow (grow-grew-grown)
- thicker
- snout
- longer
- bigger
- teeth
- become
  (become-became-become)

- sharper
- as
- learn
- more than
- growl
- hiss
- click

As they grew, they learned many things from
Mother.

But first, they learned to talk.

"Grr," Mother would say.

"Grr," the cubs would say back.

They talked with more than growls.

They talked with hisses.

They talked by clicking their teeth.

They made other sounds, too.

They also learned to play.

They loved to wrestle and to roll around.

They loved to play fight.

When they got sleepy, they snuggled with Mother.

But they were curious cubs.

They wanted to see the outdoors.

"Please, Mother?" they begged.

"Please, can we go outside?"

"Not yet," Mother said in a soft growl.

"You aren't big enough, but soon."

So the cubs played in the den.

They wrestled and rolled.

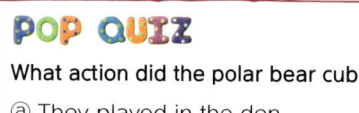

POP QUIZ

What action did the polar bear cubs not take?

ⓐ They played in the den.
ⓑ They angered Mother.

KEY WORDS

- wrestle
- roll
- play fight
- **get** (get-got-gotten)

- sleepy
- snuggle
- curious
- the outdoors

- please
- beg
- Not yet.
- soon

They napped.

They awoke and wrestled some more.

But they were tired of being inside.

They wanted to go out. Aha!

Again they asked Mother, "Please, may we go out?"

Again Mother told them, "You aren't big enough, but soon."

Every day the cubs asked.

Every day Mother said no.

KEY WORDS

- nap
- awake (awake-awoke-awoken)
- be tired of
- again
- may
- every day

- run past (run-ran-run)
- with excitement
- growling
- with joy
- leave (leave-left-left)

Then, on the day the arctic fox ran past their den,
Mother said, "Yes."

The cubs weighed about 14 kilograms now.

The cubs jumped with excitement!

They rolled together and wrestled.

They made happy growling sounds.

They danced with joy.

Today they would see the outdoors!

Today they could leave the den!

"We will go outside.

But stay close to me.

Don't run off.

I will teach you many things," Mother said.

The cubs followed Mother.

She led them into a passageway.

She led them away from the den.

They walked to the front of the cave.

The opening was covered in snow and ice.

That is why the fox couldn't see it.

"How will we get out?" the cubs asked.

"Just watch," Mother said.

Her claws broke through the ice.

She used her paws to push the snow away.

KEY WORDS

- close
- run off
- teach (teach-taught-taught)
- follow
- lead (lead-led-led)
- passageway
- away
- front
- opening
- be covered in
- get out
- watch
- break through
  (break-broke-broken)
- push away

"Wait here," she growled gently.

"I will go first.

I will be sure it is safe."

Siku and Qanuk waited.

Their black eyes shone bright.

"Let's peek out and see what Mother is doing,"

said Siku. `Aha!`

"Mother said to wait," Qanuk said.

He didn't like to disobey.

"We will wait," Siku said with a sly smile.

"But we will watch also."

The cubs crept to the cave opening and peeked out.

KEY WORDS

- wait
- gently
- be sure
- shine (shine-shone-shone)
- bright

- peek out
- disobey
- sly
- creep (creep-crept-crept)

Comprehension Quiz

A Who said what? Match each line with the right character.

❶

Mother bear

• a) "Mother said to wait."

❷

Siku

• b) "I will be sure it is safe."

❸

Qanuk

• c) "Let's peek out and see what Mother is doing."

B Fill in each blank with the right word below.

den	followed	fox	snow

❶ The cubs _____ Mother.

❷ Mother led the cubs away from the _____.

❸ The cave opening was covered in _____ and ice.

❹ That is why the _____ couldn't see it.

C Choose the best answer to each question.

❶ Which of these did the artic fox do?

a) He slipped and slid over the icy ground.

b) He blew away in the wind.

c) He peeked into the polar bears' hidden den.

d) He passed the polar bears' hidden den.

❷ Why wouldn't Mother let the cubs go outside the den?

a) They weren't big enough yet.

b) She was afraid of the fox.

c) There was too much snow.

d) She wanted to take a nap.

D Mark T for true or F for false.

❶ Mother used her nose to break through the ice. T F

❷ Siku and Qanuk were afraid to go outside. T F

❸ Mother went outside first to be sure it was safe. T F

❹ The cubs peeked outside after Mother told them to wait. T F

Humans, Wolves and Bears!

It was so bright!

Everywhere they looked they saw snowy white.

"Where is Mother?" Qanuk asked.

His voice trembled.

"I don't see her."

"Don't be scared," Siku said.

"She's right there."

He pointed to a snowdrift.

Qanuk sighed with relief.

He felt safer when Mother was near.

Mother stood on her hind legs and sniffed the air.

She was more than 213 cm tall!

She turned her head to listen.

Then she dropped her feet to the ground.

Now she stood on all fours.

Mother walked to the cave and said, "You were
supposed to wait inside.

What if there were other big bears out here?

Or humans? Or hungry wolves?

You have to listen and do what I tell you."

"What are humans?

What are wolves?"

The cubs asked.

"What other big bears?

Bigger than us?"

"You are cubs, so many animals are bigger than you," Mother said. "Full grown, we polar bears are the biggest bears on Earth.

▲ Kodiak bear

But some, like the Kodiak bear, come close. 🔺

And wolves hunt in packs.

That means there are many that hunt together.

Bears and wolves won't bother me because I'm so big.

But they all like to eat polar bear cubs."

KEY WORDS

- be supposed to + *Verb*
- what if ~?
- have to + *Verb* (have-had-had)
- full grown
- biggest
- on Earth
- Kodiak bear

- come close (come-came-come)
- hunt
- in packs
- mean (mean-meant-meant)
- bother
- because
- eat (eat-ate-eaten)

Siku and Qanuk hissed with fear.

"We're not food!"

"You will be if you don't listen and do what I say.

When I say wait, you must wait."

Fear made the cubs tremble. Aha!

Their black eyes opened wide.

"What do wolves look like?" Qanuk asked.

"They have sharp teeth.

They have four legs and thick fur.

Their tails are bushy,"

Mother said.

"Wolves sound scary."

Qanuk moved closer to

Mother.

▲ artic wolf

KEY WORDS

- with fear
- must (= have to)
- open wide

- look like
- bushy
- sound

- scary
- closer

"What are humans?" Siku asked.

Excitement brightened his eyes.

"Humans are animals on two legs.

Some humans hunt us for our warm coat.

Others use our bodies for food.

Some hunt us for sport."

"For sport?" Siku wrinkled his nose.

"What's that?"

"For fun," Mother said.

Qanuk shivered again.

"What else wants to eat us?"

"Nothing that is out here today," Mother said.

She hugged Qanuk and Siku tight.

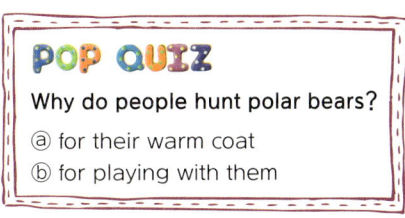

POP QUIZ

Why do people hunt polar bears?

ⓐ for their warm coat
ⓑ for playing with them

KEY WORDS

- brighten
- warm
- coat
- bodies
- sport
- wrinkle
- for fun
- shiver
- what else
- nothing
- hug
- tight

"Come out now.

It is safe for you," Mother said.

Siku and Qanuk stepped from the cave.

The day was sunny, but cold.

The wind ruffled the cubs' fur.

The cubs blinked their eyes in the bright light.

They twitched their black noses and sniffed the air.

Something smelled good!

Siku and Qanuk walked on the icy ground.

Their padded feet protected them from the cold.

The roughness of the pads helped them not to

slip or slide.

They didn't notice the cold.

Their fur protected them from

the wind.

But, oh, the smells!

A fishy smell made them

stop to sniff again.

It smelled so good!

▲ a polar bear's foot

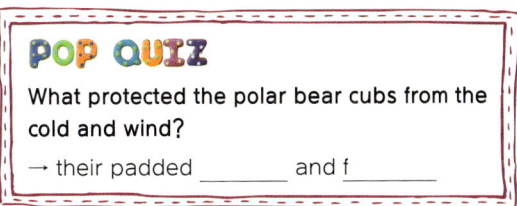

POP QUIZ

What protected the polar bear cubs from the cold and wind?

→ their padded _____ and f_____

KEY WORDS

- step from
- sunny
- blink
- twitch
- smell

- padded
- protect
- roughness
- pad
- slip

- slide (slide-slid-slid)
- notice
- fishy
- stop to + *Verb*

"You must get used to being outside our den,"
Mother said.

"In a few days, I will show you the sea.

The sea provides us food and fun."

Her growl was soft and happy.

"But for now, we will play!"

Mother played with the cubs.

She rolled in the snow.

Siku and Qanuk climbed on her back.

When she lay on her back, they climbed on her belly.  Aha!

The cubs wrestled and nipped at her ears and neck.

They had so much fun!

When Mother was tired of playing, she flopped on her belly.

She rested her head on her paws.

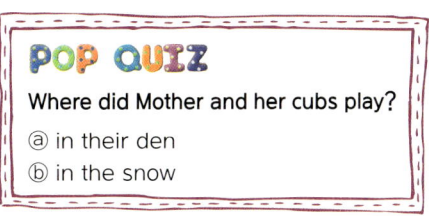

POP QUIZ

Where did Mother and her cubs play?

ⓐ in their den
ⓑ in the snow

KEY WORDS

- get used to
- in a few days
- provide
- for now

- climb
- lie on one's back (lie-lay-lain)
- belly
- nip

- have fun
- flop
- on one's belly

Siku and Qanuk wrestled a little longer.

When they grew tired, they snuggled next to

Mother for a nap.

The cold air blew their fur.

The sun warmed their noses.

The next day, they played outside again.

They took a short walk away from the den.

The next day, they took a longer walk.

Each day they walked further from the den.

Finally came the day Mother said, "Follow me.

I will show you the sea." Aha!

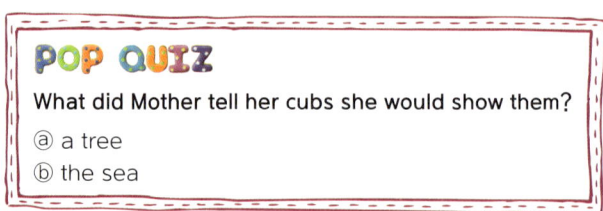

POP QUIZ

What did Mother tell her cubs she would show them?

ⓐ a tree
ⓑ the sea

KEY WORDS

- a little longer
- next to
- take a walk (take-took-taken)

- further
- finally

Comprehension Quiz

A Choose all the words that Mother used to describe a wolf.

a) bushy tail

b) pink nose

c) thick fur

d) red eyes

e) skinny legs

f) sharp teeth

g) four legs

h) small ears

B Fill in each blank with the right word below.

tremble	blinked	sniffed	protected

❶ Mother stood on her hind legs and _____ the air.

❷ Fear made the cubs _____ .

❸ The cubs _____ their eyes in the bright light.

❹ Their padded feet _____ Siku and Qanuk from the
cold.

C Choose the best answer to each question.

❶ Which of these hunts polar bears for sport?

a) foxes

b) wolves

c) humans

d) bears

❷ What protected the bears from the cold wind?

a) rolling in the snow

b) Mother snuggling them

c) their fur

d) the sunshine

D Mark T for true or F for false.

❶ Siku and Qanuk thought the fishy smell was good.　　T　F

❷ The cubs did not like to play with Mother.　　T　F

❸ Each day the bears walked further from the den.　　T　F

❹ Mother sent the cubs outside alone.　　T　F

Chapter Three

Learning to Hunt

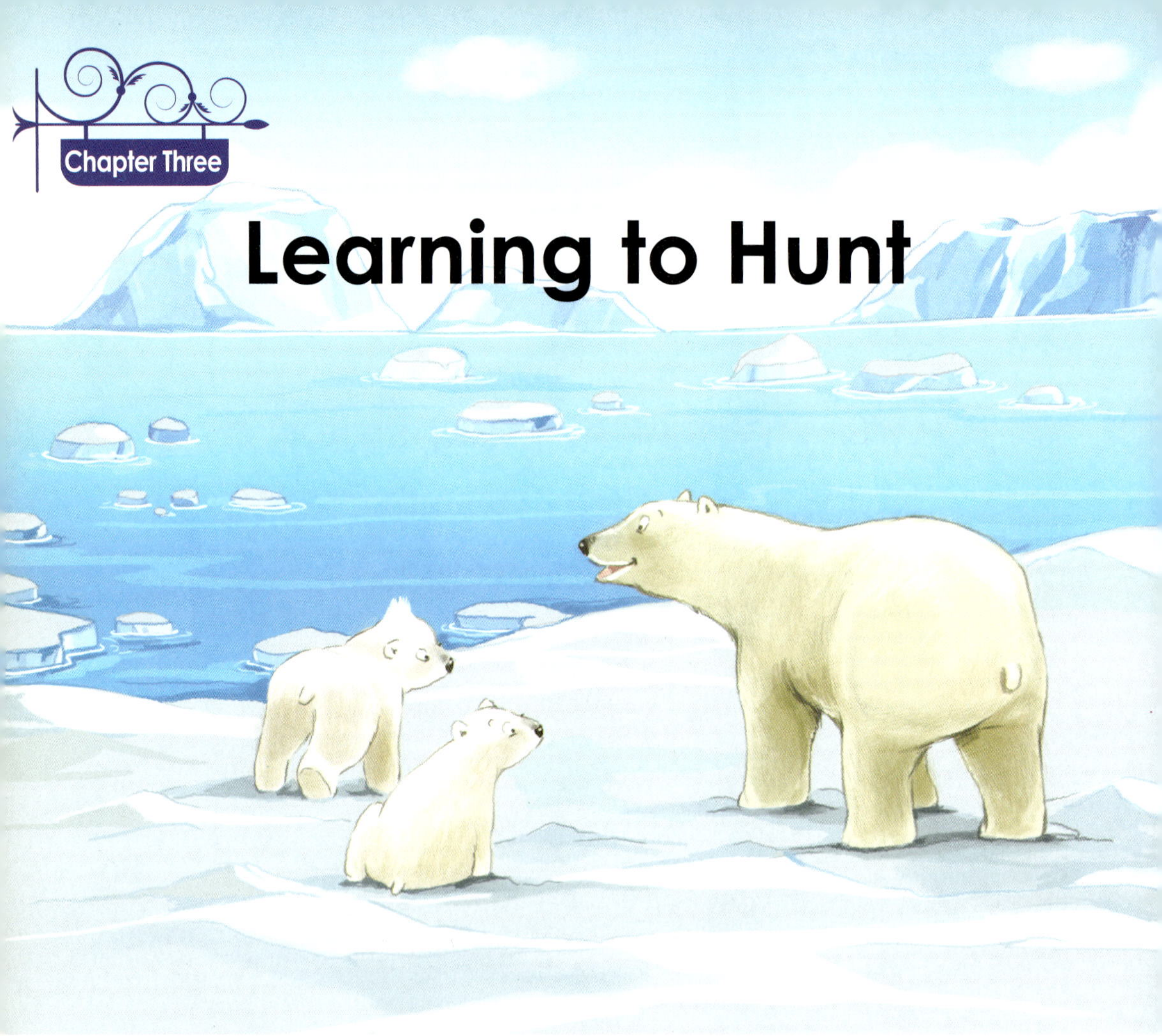

Siku and Qanuk followed Mother across the snow and ice.

Soon they stood at the edge of the ice and snow.

Slushy water lay before them.

Chunks of ice floated with the slush.

Beyond the slush the water was dark and deep.

Beyond the water lay more snow-covered ice.

Mother breathed the
salty air.

"This is the sea.

Ringed seals live in the

sea.

▲ ringed seal

They are good to eat, but

first we must catch one."

"How do we do that?"

Siku asked.

He clapped his paws and growled with delight.

Qanuk was excited too, but fearful.

What were ringed seals?

If they lived in the water, how could they be caught?

KEY WORDS

- across
- edge
- slushy
- chunk
- float
- slush

- beyond
- snow-covered
- breathe
- salty
- ringed seal
- catch (catch-caught-caught)

- clap
- with delight
- excited
- fearful

Mother lowered her head and sniffed.

She walked along the water's edge.

She sniffed some more.

Qanuk walked with care.

Siku danced along behind Mother.

Mother laid a big paw on Siku's head.

"Stop moving," she said.

"To catch a seal we must be still.

We must wait. Follow me.

When I stop, you stop."

Mother walked and sniffed.

She twitched her ears.

The cubs followed her.

When she stopped walking, so did they.

"Be very still. Do not move."

She showed them a hole in the thick ice.

"See the slushy water in the hole?

Everything beneath this ice and snow is the sea. Aha!

The seals swim below."

"They're swimming below us now?"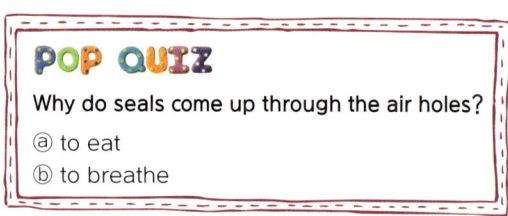

Siku's eyes shone with excitement.

"Yes," Mother said.

"That is why you must be quiet and still.

When we move, the ice cracks and the seals can hear.

It warns them.

They won't come up if they hear us."

"What is the hole for?" Qanuk asked.

Mother said, "Seals need air.

They come up through these holes to breathe.

When a seal comes up, I will catch him."

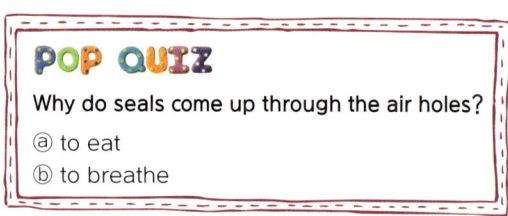

POP QUIZ

Why do seals come up through the air holes?

ⓐ to eat

ⓑ to breathe

KEY WORDS

- quiet
- crack
- warn
- come up
- need

- a block of
- stare at
- ready to + *Verb*
- pounce
- copy

- almost
- fall asleep (fall-fell-fallen)
- grumble
- boring

Mother sat still as a block of ice.

She stared at the hole, ready to pounce.

The cubs copied her.

They sat for so long that Qanuk almost fell asleep.

But not Siku.

He grumbled, "This is boring."

Mother thumped Siku on the head with her paw. "This is hunting," she growled, and looked back into the hole.

Siku rubbed his head and sighed, but he didn't complain again.

"There."

Mother's growl was low.

The sleek gray head of a seal popped up through the ice hole!

Mother pounced.

She thrust her sharp teeth into the seal's neck.

She snatched him from the hole.

Using her teeth and claws, she dragged him across the ice.

"Wahoo!" shouted Siku.

"It's time for our seal meal!"

KEY WORDS

- thump
- rub
- complain
- sleek
- pop up
- thrust
- snatch
- drag
- it is time for
- meal

Siku and Qanuk ran to Mother.

Their instincts told them it was time to eat. **Aha!**

Their bellies rumbled.

The seal meal smelled fishy and good.

They licked their chops.

Mother tore into the seal with her teeth and claws.

She was starving from the long winter when she rested and didn't eat.

KEY WORDS

- instinct
- rumble
- lick

- chop
- tear into (tear-tore-torn)
- starve

Mother polar bears rest in their dens.

They do this while waiting for their cubs to be born.

They don't eat during this time.

They live off the fat stored in their bodies.

The young cubs nurse milk from their mothers.

They nurse until they are big enough to learn how to hunt. **Aha!**

KEY WORDS

- during
- live off
- fat

- stored
- nurse
- how to + *Verb*

Now Siku and Qanuk were big enough.

They were eating their first seal!

Mother ate the fat and skin.

She left the meat for her cubs to eat. **Aha!**

Siku and Qanuk ate the seal meat.

"Mmm, good!" they said.

They ate until their bellies were round and full.

After their seal meal, Mother had another lesson for the cubs.

"It is time for a bath," she said.

"Let's go swimming!"

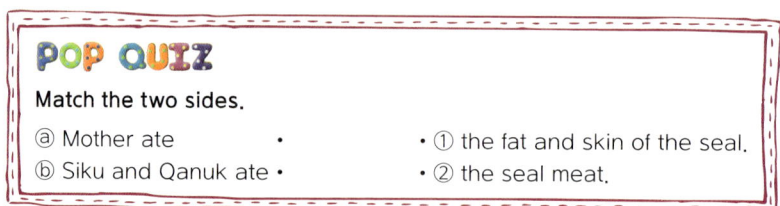

POP QUIZ

Match the two sides.

ⓐ Mother ate   •   • ① the fat and skin of the seal.
ⓑ Siku and Qanuk ate •   • ② the seal meat.

KEY WORDS

• skin
• meat

• full (↔ hungry)
• another

• lesson
• bath

A Circle the character which said each line.

❶ "This is boring."   **Mother / Siku / Qanuk**

❷ "This is hunting."   **Mother / Siku / Qanuk**

❸ "What is the hole for?"   **Mother / Siku / Qanuk**

B Mark T for true or F for false.

❶ The cubs wrestled and played while Mother hunted for a seal.   T F

❷ Mother used her teeth and claws to drag the seal across the ice.   T F

C Fill in each blank with the right word below.

deep	ice	fishy	excitement

❶ Their seal meal smelled _____ and good.

❷ Siku's eyes shone with _____ .

❸ Chunks of _____ floated with the slush.

❹ Beyond the slush the water was dark and _____ .

D Choose the best answer to each question.

❶ What did Mother want to catch and eat?

a) an arctic fox

b) a wolf

c) a fish

d) a ringed seal

❷ Which of these did Mother NOT tell the cubs to do?

a) Be still!

b) Wait!

c) Jump!

d) Stop moving!

❸ What sound warns the seals?

a) ice cracking

b) bells ringing

c) thunder rumbling

d) wind blowing

Playtime Surprise

Mother ran across the frozen ground.

Siku and Qanuk ran after her.

She stopped at the ice edge near the slush.

"Jump in. I will teach you to swim!"

Mother dove into the water.

Her big body disappeared.

A moment later, her head burst from the water.

Siku roared with delight.

He copied Mother and dove in.

He paddled his feet and pushed upward.

His head popped above the water.

KEY WORDS

- playtime
- surprise
- frozen
- run after
- **dive** (dive-dove-dived)

- disappear (↔ appear)
- a moment later
- burst
- roar
- paddle

- upward
- above
- grab

Mother waited to help him.

She floated like ice!

Siku grabbed onto Mother's back.

He called to Qanuk, "Jump in! It's fun!"

Qanuk tested the water with one paw and then the other.

He walked back and forth at the ice edge.

Crack!

The edge of the ice crumbled away.

Qanuk fell into the slushy water!

The more he tried to climb onto the ice, the more it crumbled. Aha!

Qanuk's heart raced.

He cried out for Mother.

Mother's big body moved against him.

Qanuk climbed onto Mother's back.

He held tight with his claws.

"I've got you," Mother said.

"We polar bears have lots of fat on our bodies.

It helps us float. You will learn."

Mother taught the cubs to dive, swim, and float.

They learned to clean their fur.

"Always wash after eating," Mother said.

"Wash with water or roll in the snow.

We polar bears like to be clean."

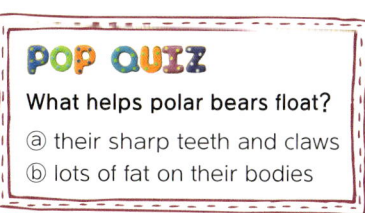

POP QUIZ

What helps polar bears float?

ⓐ their sharp teeth and claws
ⓑ lots of fat on their bodies

KEY WORDS

- test
- walk back and forth
- crumble (away)
- race
- cry out

- against
- hold (hold-held-held)
- clean
- always
- wash

After their swim, Mother found a nice spot in the snow for them to rest.

Their bellies were full.

They were tired from swimming.

They snuggled close to Mother and closed their eyes.

They didn't see the arctic fox.

He hid at the top of a snowdrift.

The smell of the leftover seal meal made him hungry.

He wanted to eat the leftovers, but he was afraid of Mother.

The fox lay down to hide and wait for the bears to leave.

POP QUIZ

What did the artic fox hope to eat?

ⓐ Qanuk and Siku
ⓑ the leftovers from the bears' seal meal

KEY WORDS

- find (find-found-found)
- spot
- top
- leftover
- be afraid of
- lie down

Siku was too excited to nap. **Aha!**

He wriggled free of Mother's arm.

He growled into Qanuk's ear, "Let's play."

Qanuk didn't want to play, but Siku's excitement was waking him up.

Soon Qanuk wriggled away from Mother, too.

The cubs crept away.

"Let's see what's on the other side of that snowdrift," Siku said.

The cubs ran through the snow.
They nipped and batted
each other with their
paws.
The brothers
laughed with
growls and
clicks of their
teeth.
They loved to
play fight.
They didn't know that play-fighting taught them
how to fight for real.
They didn't know that their play taught them
how to protect themselves.
They only knew they were having fun.

KEY WORDS

- wriggle
- free of
- wake up (wake-woke-woken)

- other side
- bat
- each other

- play-fighting
- for real

Playtime Surprise • **63**

The cubs stood at the bottom of the snowdrift and looked up.

The snowdrift reached high toward the sky.

"Let's race to the top!" Siku said.

The cubs climbed up through the ice and snow.

They slipped and slid.

If they moved slowly, their claws helped them hold on.

Up, up they went!

Higher and higher! Aha!

The arctic fox lifted his head.

He heard the cubs coming, but too late.

He couldn't move fast enough to run away.

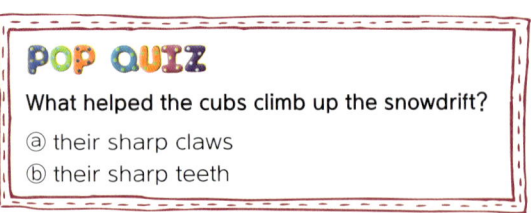

POP QUIZ

What helped the cubs climb up the snowdrift?
ⓐ their sharp claws
ⓑ their sharp teeth

KEY WORDS

- bottom
- reach
- toward
- slowly
- hold on
- higher
- late
- face to face

The cubs reached the top of the snowdrift.

They came face to face with the arctic fox!

Siku and Qanuk roared with fear.

Their hearts raced.

They stared at the animal.

It had four legs, a thick coat, and a bushy tail.

It had sharp teeth, just like a wolf!

KEY WORDS

▪ scream ▪ furry ▪ snowball

"A wolf! A wolf!" Siku cried out.

"He wants to eat us!" Qanuk screamed.

The cubs jumped away from the arctic fox.

Together they slipped, slid and fell down.

Down the snowdrift they rolled like two furry snowballs!

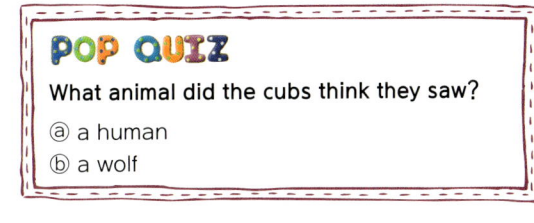

POP QUIZ

What animal did the cubs think they saw?

ⓐ a human

ⓑ a wolf

Siku and Qanuk tumbled to the bottom of the snowdrift.

They landed on top of each other.

"Oomph!" they said.

"Mother!" they screamed.

They ran to Mother, tripping and falling the whole way.

"Mother! Mother!"

The cubs wriggled under Mother's strong arms.

They hid their faces in her thick fur and their bodies shook with fear.

Mother lifted her big head.

She drew her cubs close to her body.

KEY WORDS

- tumble
- land
- trip
- the whole way
- shake (shake-shook-shaken)
- draw (draw-drew-drawn)

- silly
- sneak off
- never
- in danger
- surprised
- sure

"Silly cubs," Mother said.

"I watched you sneak off. Aha!

You were never in danger."

"But Mother!"

Qanuk cried, "There is a wolf!"

"No, there is no wolf.

There is only an arctic fox," Mother said.

"He was more scared and surprised than you!"

"Are you sure?" Siku asked.

"I am sure. The fox waits for us to leave.

He wants to eat the leftovers from our seal meal.

He is happy we ate the seal and didn't eat him!

Seals are not our only food, just our favorite.

Wait until summer.

I will teach you to catch birds and fish and find

eggs, and many other things."

Qanuk and Siku stopped shaking, but they stayed

close to Mother. Aha!

Mother squeezed her cubs tight.

She licked snow from their faces.

She growled in a way that meant, "I love you."

Qanuk and Siku snuggled closer to Mother and

copied her growl.

They wanted to be certain Mother knew that they

loved her, too.

KEY WORDS

▪ favorite ▪ squeeze ▪ be certain

POP QUIZ

What are three other kinds of food that polar bears eat?

ⓐ eggs, birds, and seashells
ⓑ birds, fish, and eggs

Chapter Four Comprehension Quiz

A Fill in each blank with the right word below.

slipped	eat	head	snowballs

❶ "He wants to _____ us!" Qanuk screamed.

❷ Together they _____, slid and fell down.

❸ They rolled like two furry _____.

❹ Mother lifted her big _____.

B Put the sentences in order.

❶ The cubs learned how to swim.

❷ The cubs climbed the snowdrift.

❸ The cubs tumbled to the bottom of the snowdrift.

❹ The cubs learned how to clean their fur.

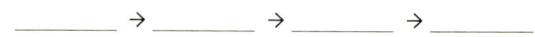

_____ → _____ → _____ → _____

C Mark T for true or F for false.

❶ Siku copied Mother and dove in. [T] [F]

❷ Qanuk climbed onto Siku's belly. [T] [F]

D Choose the best answer to each question.

❶ Why did the arctic fox hope the bears would leave?

    a) He wanted to follow them back to their den.

    b) He wanted to eat the leftovers of their seal meal.

    c) He wanted their napping spot for himself.

    d) He wanted to play in the snow.

❷ What did play-fighting teach the cubs?

    a) It taught them to fight and protect themselves for real.

    b) It taught them how to share.

    c) It taught them how to growl and hiss.

    d) It taught them how to clean their fur.

❸ Why were Siku and Qanuk so afraid of the artic fox?

    a) The fox chased them.

    b) The fox wanted to eat them for dinner.

    c) They thought the fox was a wolf.

    d) They thought the fox was a Kodiak bear.

Let's Review the Story

Fill in the blanks to review the story.

Title: Adventures of the _____ Bear Brothers

Main Characters: _____, Qanuk, and Mother polar bear

Place: The Artic

Sequence:

- The cubs were born in a snow __c_____ which is also called a den.
- When they were big enough, Mother bear brought them to the _____ to hunt for seals.
- Siku and Qanuk learned they must be very __q_____ when waiting for the seals to appear.
- After Mother caught the seal, the cubs _____ their first seal meal.
- After eating, Mother taught the cubs to __s_____, float, and wash their _____.
- Siku and Qanuk met the arctic _____ face-to-face at the top of the snowdrift.
- The cubs jumped away in fright and rolled down the snowdrift like two furry _____s .
- Mother comforted her cubs and told them the fox was not __d_____ .

Let's Think & Talk

Think about the following questions and answer them freely.

❶ Are polar bears just cute animals like Siku and Qanuk? Check and organize polar bears' true nature such as their appearance, food, behaviour, etc., then speak.

❷ Besides polar bears, what other animals live in the North Pole? Among the animals that you found, what animal interests you the most and why?

❸ Not only polar bears but also many other animals living in the North Pole are endangered. Why? Tell us what we can do to protect them.

Answers

Let's Review the Story

Title: Adventures of the **Polar** Bear Brothers

Main Characters: **Siku** , Qanuk, and Mother polar bear

Place: The Artic

Sequence:
- The cubs were born in a snow **cave** which is also called a den.
- When they were big enough, Mother bear brought them to the **sea** to hunt for seals.
- Siku and Qanuk learned they must be very **quiet** when waiting for the seals to appear.
- After Mother caught the seal, the cubs **ate** their first seal meal.
- After eating, Mother taught the cubs to **swim** , float, and wash their **fur** .
- Siku and Qanuk met the arctic **fox** face-to-face at the top of the snowdrift.
- The cubs jumped away in fright and rolled down the snowdrift like two furry **snowball**s .
- Mother comforted her cubs and told them the fox was not **dangerous** .

Smart Readers: **Wise** & **Wide**

After-reading Test

- Adventures of the Polar Bear Brothers
- Level 2
- 19 Questions

  (Vocabulary 5 / Reading Comprehension 10 /

  Sentence Structure & Grammar 4)

1. Which pair has the wrong past tense form of the listed verb?
   ① dig – dug
   ② tear – tore
   ③ mean – meant
   ④ choose – chosen

2. Which pair has the wrong comparative form of the listed adjective?
   ① big → biger
   ② long → longer
   ③ safe → safer
   ④ sharp → sharper

3. Choose all the words that express emotions.
   ① scared
   ② creep
   ③ excited
   ④ sleek

4. Which sentence has the same meaning with the one given below?

   > Wolves hunt in packs.

   ① Wolves hunt with foxes.
   ② Wolves hunt alone.
   ③ Many wolves hunt together.
   ④ Wolves hunt only in winter.

5. What is the common word for the two blanks?

> • They were tired _____ being inside.
> • He wanted to eat the leftovers, but he was afraid _____ Mother bear.

① for ② to

③ at ④ of

6. Which of these things did Mother polar bear NOT do before the cubs were born?
   ① She built a den inside a snowdrift.
   ② She shared her den with other mother bears.
   ③ She used her strong paws to move the snow.
   ④ She used her sharp claws to dig into the ice.

7. Who raises polar bear cubs?
   ① both the father and mother
   ② the father polar bear
   ③ the mother polar bear
   ④ someone other than the mother or father

8. How tall is Mother polar bear when she stands on two feet?
   ① less than 200 cm tall
   ② more than 213 cm tall
   ③ 230 cm tall
   ④ 610 cm tall

9. Polar bears make sounds to communicate with each other. Which of these sounds do they NOT make?

① hisses

② clicking of teeth

③ meows

④ growls

10. Mother polar bear said, "Some hunt us for sport." What does "for sport" mean?

① for protection

② for fun

③ for lesson

④ for food

11. Why do the seals come through the hole in the ice?

① to play

② to eat

③ to meet other seals

④ to breathe

12. What is it that helps polar bears float?

① ice chunks

② slush

③ their fur

④ their fat

13. Who was the artic fox most afraid of?
    ① a seal
    ② a wolf
    ③ the cubs
    ④ Mother polar bear

14. What did the polar bear cubs climb?
    ① a tree
    ② a snowdrift
    ③ an ice wall
    ④ a snowball

15. What did the polar bear cubs think they saw on a snowdrift?
    ① a fox
    ② a seal
    ③ a wolf
    ④ a human

※ Choose the wrong part of the sentence. (16~17)

16.
> Fear made the cubs to tremble.
> ①   ②   ③   ④

17.

Everything <u>beneath</u> this <u>ice and</u> snow <u>are</u> <u>the sea</u>.
          ①   ②   ③ ④

※ Choose the correct order of the given words to complete each sentence. (18~19)

18.

Siku was (to, too, nap, excited) .

① to excited too nap

② to nap too excited

③ too excited to nap

④ too excited nap to

19.

They nurse until they are (learn, big, to, enough)
how to hunt.

① to learn enough big

② enough big to learn

③ to learn big enough

④ big enough to learn

Memo

Memo

Lisa Ricard Claro

Lisa Ricard Claro is an award-winning short story author with published articles and stories spanning multiple media. Her first adult fiction novel is scheduled for publication. She resides in Atlanta, Georgia with her husband, two dogs and two cats, and dreams of one day living at the beach. Writing is Lisa's passion, and she loves creating fiction and nonfiction stories for both adults and children.

 Smart Readers Wise & Wide 2-4

Adventures of the Polar Bear Brothers

Written by Lisa Ricard Claro
Illustrated by Donghun Kim

First published June 2015
Second printing June 2022

Publisher: Kyudo Chung
Editors: Juyon Choi, Kyunghee Jang, Jiyeong Park
Designers: Eunhee Lee, Elim

Published and distributed by
Happy House, an Imprint of DARAKWON, Inc.
Darakwon Bldg., 211 Munbal-ro, Paju-si, Gyeonggi-do, 10881, Republic of Korea
Tel: 82-2-736-2031(ext. 250)   Fax: 82-2-732-2037
Homepage: www.ihappyhouse.co.kr

ISBN: 978-89-6653-194-3 18740 / 978-89-6653-156-1 18740(set)

[Components]
• 1 Audio CD (Recording Studio: Aram)
• Answer Keys & Korean Translation: Free download at www.ihappyhouse.co.kr